CHATTO POETS FOR THE YOUNG
A Parliament of Birds

CHATTO POETS FOR THE YOUNG

General Editor: LEONARD CLARK

A Parliament of Birds

BY

JOHN HEATH-STUBBS

1975

CHATTO & WINDUS

LONDON

Published by
Chatto & Windus Ltd
40 William IV Street
London WC2N 4DF

*

Clarke, Irwin & Co. Ltd
Toronto

For

SARAH *and* REBECCA

ISBN 0 7011 5075 0

© John Heath-Stubbs 1975

Printed in Great Britain by
REDWOOD BURN LIMITED, TROWBRIDGE . ESHER

1 0 0 1 9 6 5 2 2 3

Contents

THE EAGLES

Where the Roman legions tramped
Their brazen eagle-standards went before,
While, at the army's rear,
The feathered eagles soared, and waited.

"They make a desert and they call it peace."
Victorious, in the war-god's shrine,
The dedicated brazen eagles stand;
About the wasted land
The feathered eagles fight and tear.

THE KESTREL

The small falcon, with sharp pointed wings,
Hangs poised in air, standing against the gale:
The intense lens of his unwinking eye
Is focused on the fields below, to mark
Each slightest stir or scurry in the grass.

And, as in Egypt, this is Horus-Ra,
Lord of the Morning, sacred
Emblem of Pharaoh's kingship,
Royal Bird of the Sun.

THE TAWNY OWL

Autumn night, a great shiny moon —
Owls cry and cry over the sleeping farms:
"To-whoo! To-whoo! To-whoo!
Poor Jenny Hoolet's feet are a-cold!"

A mouse
Sneaks out to a corn-stack, begins
To nibble the spilt grain. Suddenly,
On noiseless downy wings, with never a whisper, Death
Swoops down from the frosty air.

THE HOOPOE

A rare one with us —
King Solomon's messenger to the Queen of Sheba;
Sheltered that wise king
From the heat of the midday sun.

He offered a reward — they asked
For crowns of gold.

Poor silly birds — soon everybody harried them
With sticks and stones, until the king
Turned the gold crowns to feathers.
A feathered crown is best.

THE TREE-CREEPER

I saw a little mouse
Run up a tree — then twitch
Out pointed delicate wings,
And flitter away on the breeze.

THE NUTHATCH

Slate-blue above, buff below,
Descends a tree-trunk upside down,
Punctures a nut with his sharp chisel-bill,
And whistles clear and cheeky,
Shrill as a schoolboy.

THE RAVENS

Tolls the bell, hour upon hour —
Always ravens at the Tower.

Glossy and black the plumes we preen,
And black the sights that we have seen.

Tolls the bell, hour upon hour —
Always ravens at the Tower.

Clarence drowned, the little princes —
The shadow of Crookback Dick advances.

Tolls the bell, hour upon hour —
Always ravens at the Tower.

Headless the Bullen and Howard here,
Headless Raleigh, and headless More.

Tolls the bell, hour upon hour —
Always ravens at the Tower.

When we fly hence, the Tower shall crumble,
The city be lost, and the realm tumble.

Tolls the bell, hour upon hour —
Always ravens at the Tower.

THE MAGPIE

Feather-pated tattling Margaret Pie
Would not go into Noah's Ark, we are told:
She sat on the roof and chattered in the rain.

On another occasion she said
"I think I will only go into half-mourning."
The occasion was the Crucifixion.
She's worn it ever since.

THE GREEN WOODPECKER

He is the green-plumed popinjay of our northern woods,
Lunatic laugher of spring, destroyer
Of the ants' citadel.
He is loved by the Thunder God, and the nymphs
Of the druid oak-groves.

THE CUCKOO

The cuckoo and the warty toad
Digest the woolly caterpillars:

Only their toughened stomachs
Can cope with those poisonous hairs.

The cuckoo is footloose, irresponsible —
He scorns domestic cares,

And parks his ugly offspring on
His dupes, dunnock and titlark.

He's free to sing all day
His two-note song to his grey light-of-love;

And she replies, bubbling
Like water from a wide-necked bottle.

The cuckoo is a graceless, greedy bird —
And yet we love him still:

He told us spring had come. And all our days
We will remember cuckoo-time.

THE KINGFISHER

When Noah left the Ark, the animals
Capered and gambolled on the squadgy soil,
Enjoying their new-found freedom; and the birds
Soared upwards, twittering, to the open skies.
But one soared higher than the rest, in utter ecstasy,
Till all his back and wings were drenched
With the vivid blue of heaven itself, and his breast
    scorched
With the upward-slanting rays of the setting sun.
When he came back to earth, he had lost the Ark;
His friends were all dispersed. So now he soars no more;
A lonely bird, he darts and dives for fish,
By streams and pools — places where water is —
Still searching, but in vain, for the vanished Ark
And rain-washed terraces of Ararat.

THE MUTE SWAN

The white swan makes a fine picture,
And looks as if he knew it. He arches
His delicate neck to quiz
That other swan which swims,
Upside down beneath him.

Richard Lionheart it was
Brought these swans here, from Cyprus where
They floated on moats which lapped
Proud castles of the royal Lusignan,
Among the olive and the citrus groves.

THE WHOOPER SWAN

These are Apollo's birds, straight-necked and yellow-
    billed,
Nomads of the northern waste, who swept
Southward, with high clear song, to visit
Delphi's oracular shrine, or where
The power divine had fixed
Delos, once wandering, in mid-sea deep.

PR 6015 . E284

LIBRARY BOOK SUGGESTION

(BLOCK CAPITALS ONLY)

Date of request

AUTHOR (Surname first) HEATH-STUBBS, John

TITLE A Parliament of Birds

PUBLISHER Chatto & Windus

	No of Copies	
	Date of Publication	1975

Recommended by — Dept

Reserve for

Price		ISBN							
HBK									
PBK									
Branch 000	Loan 09	Fund							
Branch 000	Loan	Fund							
Branch 000	Loan	Fund							
Control No		6 0 2 0 3 4							

LIBRARY USE

Order No A 4 6 5

Date Ordered

Supplier DON - Moore

Details found
Libertas ✗
Card cat. ✗

WRL

-7 AUG 2000

Record bought
Ⓨ N

THE WILD GEESE

A pack of hounds, in full cry,
Up in the clouds. The Dark Huntsman
Pursues the poor lost souls
Until the end of time.

Wild geese passing over.

THE SHELDRAKE

Armorial bird, he bears his quarterings
Upon his wing, half goose half duck,

And lives in a feudal castle, perhaps?
No, foxgoose, in a rabbit burrow.

THE STORM PETREL

Far out at sea, a little dark bird,
No bigger than a sparrow. It teeters over the waves,
The troughs and crests, paddling with its feet,
Seeming to walk like Peter
Upon Gennasaret.

Is it a land bird that has lost its way? No,
But this is Mother Carey's chicken,
Harbinger of the storm.

O Mother Carey, green-toothed hag,
Mistress of the hurricane, your herds
The mighty choirs of singing whales, be lenient
To sailors and trawlermen, all who ply their way
Through dirty weather, over the hungry deep.

THE CORMORANT

A lone black crag stands offshore,
Lashed by the flying spray. Gorged from his fishing-
    foray
With long hooked beak and greenish glistering eye,
A cormorant, like a heraldic bird,
Spreads out dark wings, two tattered flags, to dry.

GREAT BLACK-BACKED GULLS

Said Cap'n Morgan to Cap'n Kidd:
"Remember the grand times, Cap'n, when
The Jolly Roger flapped on the tropic breeze,
And we were the terrors of the Spanish Main?"
And Cap'n Kidd replied: "Aye when our restless souls
Were steeped in human flesh and bone;
But now we range the seven seas, and fight
For galley scraps that men throw overboard."

Two black-backed gulls, that perched
On a half-sunken spar —
Their eyes were gleaming-cold and through
The morning fog that crept upon the grey-green waves
Their wicked laughter sounded.

THE WOODCOCK

This mysterious, softly-mottled creature
Is a little bug-eyed monster.

His ears are in front of his eyes, to hear
The turning worms he probes
With his sensitive, soft-tipped bill.

The brain pushed so far back, that people thought
He had no brain at all.

They come in, surreptitiously, from the sea,
Arriving on migration,
And scuttle away into the undergrowth,
Beneath the great bright moon.

And people also thought
They could fly up into that shining orb.

THE WATERHEN

The lily pads, and the lily's pale chalice
Float on the still pool. A dragon-fly
Darts above, a miniature
Futuristic aeroplane.

Demure, in black and grey,
With white beneath the tail, and that touch
Of scarlet on the brow and bill, the waterhen
Slips through the reeds, on delicate greenish feet.

THE OYSTERCATCHER

They say in the Highlands and the Western Isles —
This tale was made by men who knew
What being harried and pursued could mean — that
   Jesus,
Fleeing the malice of his enemies,
Went down to the wild shore, to find a cave to hide in.
But the sea-pies, flying
About the limpet-covered reef, with clear bright calls,
Took pity on him there; and in their scarlet beaks
Brought kelp and tangle to cover him completely.
The ruthless foe went by. And for that season
His cup of suffering passed.
                      Therefore the oystercatcher
Is of good fortune and well seen of men,
Running at the tide's edge
Upon the cockle and the mussel banks.

THE GREAT BUSTARD

On Salisbury Plain, by the great standing pillars
Of Avebury or Stonehenge — temples reared

To Sun, and changing Moon, and all
The glittering cohorts of the arching sky —

Among the scattered mounds, the Long and the
    Round Barrows,
Sepulchres of now-forgotten chieftans,

Noblest of running birds, the bustard once
Stalked before his wives, moustachioes bristling.

The bustards are all gone — they'll come no more:
Much too easy to shoot, much too good to eat.

On Salisbury Plain the military
Has taken over now, with tanks and guns,

Precision instruments of death — and human beings
Are much too easy to shoot.

THE PHEASANT

Cock-pheasant crows in the English wood,
Then struts into the clearing — magnificent,
With emerald casque, russet and white and black;
For he was made for Asiatic landscapes —
His lineage is of Colchis, land of the Golden Fleece,
Or further eastward where
Slant-eyed Chinese limned him,
With swift sure brush strokes, on their scrolls of silk.

THE HOUSE SPARROW

Citizen Philip Sparrow, who likes
To build and breed about our habitations —
    The little birds that fly through the city smoke —

Prolific, adaptable, bold,
Untidy, cheerfully vocal —
    The little birds that quarrel in the eaves —

Grant him his right of freedom and, of your charity,
His dole of crumbs and kitchen scraps —
    The little birds that stand in the eye of God.

22

THE YELLOWHAMMER

This small bird, yellow as the never-
Out-of-blossom gorse (when gorse
Is out of blossom, kissing's out of fashion.)
Reiterates his little
"A little bit of bread and no cheese!"
Through the long summer days,
When other birds are silent.

When I was younger, days were longer,
Summers were warmer, and always
The yellowhammer's song.

THE CORN BUNTING

Beside a field of grain, perched on a telephone wire,
Through the relentless August heat the dumpy
Undistinguished bird repeats
His only song. The sound is rather like
The chinkering of a rusty chain.

Each one does his best, I hope:
Each one has his talent.

THE NIGHTJAR

Summer twilight — the sun has left the sky.
A faint glow lingers. Silvery Venus
Beams a message from its alien world.
On the tall grasses points of green fire,
Elf-eyes. The glow-worms hoist their lanterns,
Love-signals for their wandering knights. Listen, a
    voice —
Intermittent whirring, spinning, churning. Almost
    invisible,
A night-jar lies along the length of a bough,
Mottled, with frog-like gape. Then snaps his wings,
And flits along the glade, pursuing
The soft, furry moth, and the blundering dor.

THE SWIFT

There is no creature (except, perhaps,
The angels) so wholly native to
The upper air. His tiny feet
Cannot walk on ground, can cling only.
The wisps and straws he needs to build his nest
He snatches in mid-air. He even sleeps
Borne up by the rising thermals.

This black screamer, rushing at evening
Above our cities, is kin
To the tropical humming bird, who can fly backwards
Out of the great flower-bells
In the Amazonian forest.

THE SWALLOW

The swallow has returned, and we can say for sure
That spring is here, and summer will follow after.
All through our winter, around an African kraal
His steel-blue pinnions flickered; now he's flown back
Thousands of miles, over the seas and mountains,
To build once more his nest in an English barn —
Hooray for the swallow and the weather he brings
    with him!

THE MISSEL-THRUSH

February brings its storms and rain,
Flooding the side-walks and the dirt-choked drain;
Into the north-west wind a missel-thrush
Shouts his defiance from a bare-twigged bush,
Sprinkling the air with notes that seem as bright
As crocus, or the yellow aconite.

THE BLACKBIRD

"Sooty-plumed blackbird with your golden bill,
Why is your song so sweet and clear and mellow?"
"I lubricate my voice with slugs and snails."
"And sometimes cherries, too?" "Well, do you grudge
    me those —
Who pay you richly with a summer tune?"

THE SPOTTED FLYCATCHER

He takes his stance on a gate-post
All the long day; makes quick
Excursions up into the air —
Snip! Snap! Snap! Snip! — snatching
The dancing flies out of their element.

THE GREAT TIT

Sir Thomas Titmouse
Has come into our garden. He likes
Suet, beef-bones, peanuts, and maybe
Half a coconut suspended.

On the first fine day of the year
He will favour you with a song — just two notes,
Up and down, like sharpening a saw.
Not much of a song, you say? It is Hope's clarion
Annually renewed.

THE PIED WAGTAIL

Polly Dishwasher is down by the stream,
Dipping and dabbling, and flirting her long tail,

In her neat black and white, black and grey
Domestic service uniform.

Her mistress is a curmudgeonly,
Sour-faced, elderly fairy,

Whose third cousin was, they say,
Lady-in-waiting to Queen Mab.

She allows her one Wednesday afternoon off a month,
Home at sunset, and *no* followers.

THE HEDGE SPARROW
Feeding a cuckoo in the nest

"My son is an infant prodigy, who'll doubtless
Make his mark in the world.
But then, though I say it myself,
Mr. Hedge Sparrow and I
Are remarkable parents.

Mrs. Meadow Pipit down the road
Says her chick is prodigious too.
The vanity of the creature!"

THE ROBIN

(i)
The north wind blows, a leaden
Sky lowers above;
Snow, snow everywhere
Over the grudging ground.
Upon a leafless bough
A solitary robin sings:
"Oh babes in the wood, poor babes in the wood —
Don't you remember the babes in the wood?"

(ii)
Cock-robin in spring, his breast
Is a flag of aggression, which says
"Get out! This front garden is mine,
These are my worms, my nesting-site, my hen-bird!
Get out! Be off! I'm warning you!" — his song
A splutter of defiant rage.

THE WREN

The pygmy troglodyte, with tail cocked,
Runs through his caves, which are
The twisted roots and debris of the copse;
Then gives a loud burst of sudden song,
And stops as suddenly. Like a clockwork bird
Someone has wound up.

THE STONECHAT

This little ruddy bird of stony places,
Too rough for the harrow,
Has the chink of pebbles inside his throat
To serve him for a song.

THE REED WARBLER

And you, skilful basket maker,
Who harbour in the whispering sedge
And vocal reeds — the inconsequential
Loquacious prattle of waters
Has flowed into your song.

THE WOOD WARBLER, THE WILLOW WARBLER, & THE CHIFFCHAFF

I thought the leaves had come to life;
It was the leaf-green birds.

I thought the green leaves
Had found their singing voice — the high sweet trill,
The tinkling chimes dying away,
The soft *zip-zap* of earliest spring.

THE NIGHTINGALE

The inconspicuous nightingale
Is not so rare as you perhaps may think,

Being not at all averse from
Home Counties conurban shrubberies,

And sings at least as much
By day as through the night —

Such is the urgency, when May-time rules,
Of finding a mate, defending territory:

The common motives for song, as for all birds.
So much for poets' fancies then?

And yet, and yet, and yet. . .
That clear high *terew,* that long crescendo,

The dark sob in the throat — these simulate
The tones of human passion,

Telling of tragic sorrows, Greek and unassuageable,
Or, as the Persians told, he sang

With wounded heart, pressing against a thorn,
In love with the opening rose, that silken-petalled jilt,

Who flings her perfume to the morning breeze —
With beauty that fades, beauty that is eternal.

THE BLACKCAP

The Southern folk can boast their nightingale,
    Which chirrups a high-class tune,
Just like Madame Adelina Patti,
    Under the summer moon;

But the Northern nightingale, he is the blackcap,
    Warbling the leaves between,
Where the oak and the ash and the bonny birk-tree
    Flourish and grow green.

O brave blackcap, O blithe blackcap
    You sing so rich and clear
In the oak and the ash and the bonny ivy
    At the season of the year.

THE SKYLARK

"There's a sparrer up there," said the Cockney boy,
On his first day in the country,
"And 'e can't get up, and 'e can't get down,
And 'e don't arf make a song about it!"

That is one way of looking at it!
Shelley, of course, saw different.

THE TURTLE DOVE

One day, one day,
After the eagles of war have preyed,
When the flowers appear on the earth, and it is spring —
The time of the singing of birds — the turtle dove
(As when the first flood-waters fell away)

Will build her nest in the heart of the peaceful grove.